# Residue

BY FLY Musiq

First Printing 2015

Bobo, Cierra T.

Residue

ISBN-13: 978-1508705659

ISBN-10: 1508705658

www.flymusiq.com

# DEDICATION

This book is dedicated to women like me who desire to or have already overcome sexual immorality. You will find that throughout these pages I am very transparent about my own struggles in hopes that someone else will be empowered to confront their sexual past and present. This is not a book of do's and don'ts. The goal isn't to convey guilt, but knowledge, grace, and hope. My prayer is that this book inspires you to think, reconsider, decide, forgive, forget, and, if necessary, change. I have not mastered life, but I'm determined to stay connected to the Master of Life. May God's grace comfort and restore broken hearts and bruised souls.

# CONTENTS

# ACKNOWLEDGEMENTS

You are the beat of my heart, the peace in my soul, the source of my being, and the love of my life. God, thanks for being committed to the voyage of life with me. I'm truly grateful that I don't have to travel this road alone. I love you, Jesus.

Writing this book challenged me to remain accountable to my beliefs and commitment to celibacy before marriage. Therefore, I thank God for sending me a husband that was committed to travel the journey of celibacy with me. We recently got married, and had sex for the first time on our wedding night. The journey wasn't always easy or perfect, but I learned a lot along the way. Don Bobo, I love you beyond words and I am grateful that you waited for me.

I thank God for such a loving and supportive family. I love the Reed, Zackery, and Sparks families dearly. Thanks for always believing in me. Next, I want to publicly acknowledge my team. They are a committed and faithful group of people. A special thanks goes out to Antwon Davis, Ereka Thomas, Pallena Foreman, Francine White, DeLandria Staton, Vanessa Johnson, Dawn Adolph, Veronica, Grace Jordan, De'Marcus Allen, Eugenia Johnson, and Mike Lewis. I truly appreciate you guys.

Finally, I would like to thank my extended families: World Changers Church International, No Losing Inc., The

King Center, and Wellspring Living. I am truly grateful for the wisdom that you continually pour into me and the opportunity to be a part of these amazing teams.

# TESTIMONIAL

As a former prostitute, people often ask me if I regret some of the things that have happened to me in my past days. There was a time where I lived in complete depression. I had consistent flashbacks, nightmares, and many mournful hours. The emotional pain was potent. I had completely allowed Satan to take a toll on my heart and rob me of my joy. I was his personal puppet, and oh did he have his fun with me! But after receiving tons of inner healing and an earful of powerful testimonials from my mentor & friend Cierra "FLY" Reed, I can honestly say that I have ZERO regrets. My past is what made me the strong woman that I am today. My past was only a heinous beginning to a dominant ending. Cierra is a true spirit-lifter whom I greatly thank for playing a major role in my life.

#Blessed

-Honesty Ballard,·
19 years old

# FOREWORD

The first time I met Fly, I knew I was in the presence of a dynamic young woman. I have never seen someone with more determination to change a generation than Fly Musiq. Fly has seen firsthand the damage that occurs in the lives of many of the youth she meets. Fly realizes this trauma can certainly paralyze its victims or build defensive walls eventually crumble into self-destruction. Fly came to a point where sitting in her own RESIDUE was no longer an option. Instead, she created a dialogue that helps lead youth to face their situations and move beyond the RESIDUE of their circumstances.

Fly's hands-on work with hundreds of youth is making a huge impact in Atlanta. Her music and radio programs reinforce her message of moving beyond the RESIDUE. Because Fly has walked alongside hundreds of young girls and young people with such great compassion and wisdom, she is completely qualified to write this guide so that many more can overcome the RESIDUE of their lives and experience HOPE. RESIDUE is comprehensive message that confronts the messiness of life, but it doesn't leave you there. Fly's frank narrative will challenge you to realize that no matter what you've experienced and the scars of life you've encountered, there is freedom beyond that pain. Fly gives practical and very challenging advice (maybe advice you think will be impossible to follow). However, her wise words will lead you to leave the RESIDUE behind and reach for a bright future.

Fly's passion is contagious. I believe reading this book will change you forever!


Mary Frances Bowley
Founder, Wellspring Living

# INTRODUCTION

Sex is beautiful thing; however, when mishandled it can be the cause of more pain than pleasure. Society consistently promotes the pleasant aspects of having sex, but fails to understand that unhealthy sex is the root cause of several cultural epidemics, including fatherlessness, the spread of sexually transmitted diseases, sex trafficking, molestation, and various internal issues. Unhealthy sex is any form of sex that occurs outside the framework of its original context. The impact that it has on women is severe.

Sex is beyond a physical act for women; it's also emotional and spiritual. Therefore, we view sex as an expression of love. When a man doesn't view sex the same way, it opens the door for women to doubt their value. A woman that doubts her worth is a broken woman. When a woman isn't whole in her emotions, she makes unwise decisions based on how she feels, and that is dangerous because emotions are temporary. Ultimately, her need to feel valued could cause her to seek love through sex, but sex isn't the cure for wounded emotions or insecurities. If anything, it can make it worse.

Living in a society where women are pressured to live up to a certain image creates feelings of competitiveness among us. These days, many women feel like they have to go out of their way to be the best dressed, the most fashionable, the most successful, the most attractive, and the best sexual performers. When a woman's confidence rests in her looks or her ability to perform, she will never rest in the assurance of her true worth. God never intended for women to compete or compare themselves with one another. He never wanted them to work to earn the respect or love of a man. He led by example by not requiring us to work for His love. This lets us know that he created us to be honored, respected, protected, cherished, and (most importantly) loved by men. However, when a woman doesn't understand God's purpose and love for her, she will lower her standards.

Women must understand that they are precious in the sight of God. They are created to do more than give physical pleasure to a man. However, when a woman makes a decision to indulge in sex outside of its proper context, she opens herself up to the possibility of being left with sexual residue.

I wrote this book to inspire and uplift my sisters. We are queens, and it's time to hold one another accountable to the greatness inside of us. In order to accomplish this goal, I share my own sexual struggles, victories, and failures in this book. I am neither better nor different from you. However, I have been blessed to receive awesome wisdom and revelation that I have chosen to share. You no longer have to be bound to sexual residue. Choose to be free today. #Residue

# Chapter 1

# Sexual High

Do you know who you are? Yes, that's such a simple question, but the answer often proves to be complicated. Nevertheless, if you don't know the true answer, it can be the root cause of countless issues. Truthfully, it's not a question that you can ask yourself once. This is a question that you have to keep asking yourself frequently. It is easy to lose sight of who you are in a world that is consistently redefining women and their worth. Therefore, you have to make a conscious decision to stay true to the essence of who you were created to be. When you were never taught your value, it is easy to get lost as you search for fulfillment in things that feel good. However, you must realize that everything that feels good isn't equipped to define you. Sex can be both emotionally and physically pleasing, but your vagina is not where your value lies. While this is easily said, it is tough to decipher at times.

There is one trait that all women share: the need to be loved. That's not a bad thing. We were created by a God who is love and who designed us out of an expression of His love. Therefore, that explains our desire to be loved and have it expressed to us. Every woman doesn't have the same love language or receive love from the same acts of display. Still, we all need it. When you don't position yourself to receive it from your creator, you feel incomplete, and incomplete people have a void in their hearts and souls. When there is a void in our hearts, it's our natural instinct to turn to something that makes us feel complete. Unfortunately, many women have turned to unhealthy relationships and sex to fill the void. The attention a man gives a woman during sex makes us feel desired and loved and, quite frankly, that feeling is amazing. I know because I've felt it on numerous occasions. That's why when a woman is dating a guy, if she has any questions in her mind about how he feels about her she becomes willing to give him her body in order to feel assured. When he takes her body, it feels like he is taking and choosing her. That's not the case for men. It is possible for some men to have sex with you and not emotionally or spiritually desire you. They indulge in your body because it brings them sexual satisfaction, not because they desire you. Having sex with a women isn't a sign that a man wants to be with a woman, commitment is. If a man truly desires and wants you, he will commit. If he doesn't commit, it's because he doesn't desire you. However, that will not stop him from having sex with you.

Nevertheless, when you know who you are and that you are shaped in the love of God, you aren't moved by the fact that a man doesn't desire you, and you don't go looking for a man to want you. You simply revel in who God made you to be while enjoying the pleasantries of life. But for a woman that doesn't know these things, she can easily become addicted to the search for sexual highs.

A woman that is addicted to sexual highs often finds herself full of questions such as: "Is this real love?", "Does he really care about me?", and "Am I his only woman?". You would think that women wouldn't have sex with a man when their spirit isn't at peace concerning those questions, but they do. Just like a crack cocaine addict who gets high despite knowing the risks of overdosing or doing jail time if caught because the drug use is gratifying, women continue to have risky sex because of the physical pleasure and feelings of being desired that sex brings.

3

The dangerous thing about sexual highs is that they may eventually turn into lows. Every high is bound to come down, and it will usually cost you something once it does. For many women, it costs them their peace, their health, their confidence, and their liberty. Nothing is worth any of those things. Having a peace of mind is priceless.

Peace gives you the strength to live. When your spirit is uneasy, it's difficult to enjoy life. We are only given one body during our lifetime, and keeping it healthy is essential. Don't shorten your experience on earth searching for fulfillment in something that can never fulfill you. Good health is a gift from God. It's a blessing to be healthy. Therefore, don't jeopardize your health by making unwise sexual decisions. I know that there is a world campaign promoting practicing safe sex. I totally agree with that. However, I believe that the safest form of sex is saving sex until marriage. Still, I am aware that you may be sexual active already. That doesn't make you a horrible person. God's love for you is the same whether you are a virgin or not. The purpose of this book is not to compare great women with those who aren't. The words on these pages are meant for education, understanding, grace, and most importantly an expression of God's love for you. God establishes certain boundaries in life, not to be a mean schoolmaster but to protect you. It's like the parent that tells a child not to run around the pool. To the child at times it can seem like your parents are trying to stop you from having fun, but that's not the case. Your parents brought you to the pool because they wanted you to enjoy it, but they know that if they don't advise you on the pool guidelines, then the very thing that was meant for your pleasure can harm or even kill you. That's exactly how God is. He created sex for two reasons: reproduction and to express love and passion between a man and woman. Sex was created to be pleasurable and fun. However, if the guidelines aren't followed it too can harm or kill you. Therefore, God advises you from a place of love. He doesn't want to withhold any good thing from you, but He also doesn't want anything to harm you. Saving sex until marriage lessens the risk of contracting a disease or being used for your body. This guideline was put into place as a guard to protect your heart, body, and soul.

The best advice that I can give any woman, regardless of her past, is to practice celibacy until you are married. Your beliefs will be tested and often challenged in the process. However, when your confidence is in God you will have the courage to withstand those challenges. Confidence and security are the keys to successful celibacy. When your confidence is not stable in God love and promises for your life, fear will cause you to compromise your values. Then, you become vulnerable and more likely engage in unhealthy sexual activities. Unfortunately, unhealthy sexual experiences when a woman feels bound or helpless, she is less likely to make decisions that will move her forward into her purpose or destiny. Unhealthy sex has the ability to leave you emotionally bound to that encounter and cause you to get caught up in a cycle of stagnant sexual repetition. You'll become dependent on sex, even when you know deep within that it's not the right situation for you to be in. That is when you have to place sex back into its proper context. Sex is not a physical, emotional, or spiritual need. It is a gift given within the institution of marriage. There is a huge difference between a gift and a need. You can't survive without the things you need, but gifts simply make surviving more pleasurable. Therefore, never allow yourself to become dependent on something that you are able to survive without. The emotional highs that sex provides cause you to think that it is a need. Don't be deceived. You can survive without having sex. Don't become so caught up in sex that you allow the repercussions of it to hinder you from walking in your God-given potential on this earth. You were created to reign as queens on this earth, which means you were never supposed to be bound by anything. When a queen doesn't exercise her authority, her kingdom is at stake. Your kingdom is the territory, idea, business plan, company, design, task, invention, or industry that God called for you to reign in and make a positive mark on. When a woman doesn't move forward into her purpose, she never becomes truly satisfied with life because her spirit recognizes that she isn't walking in her true position on the earth. God deposited the seed of everything that you needed in life inside of your spirit. It is up to us to allow Him to move into our spirits and water the seed so it can flourish into great harvest. We were all placed on the earth to leave a positive impact on it, and that impact will happen within the context of your purpose. You are significant! When you don't fulfill your purpose, you never truly experience what life is all about. Therefore, it's vital for a woman to feel free to fulfill her greatest potential as the queen that God made her to be. Don't allow bad sexual experiences be the reason why you don't awaken to who you were destined to be. You can be delivered from being bound to sexual highs. There is freedom in God's love for you. When you realize how much God loves you unconditionally, it liberates you. You recognize that you know longer have to do things to earn approval or to feel significant. In His eyes you are already approved. When I really began to comprehend that, I became bolder in who I was and my right to deny others access to my body. I got the revelation that my body, spirit, and soul were purchased by the expensive blood of Jesus. If Christ thought enough of me to die for me, then I must be extremely valuable. That understanding caused me to become courageous in moments when I had to say no to a man when asked to have sex. Jesus became my confidence. Ultimately, your freedom from sexual bondage rests in your confidence in God's love for you.

I tell the young ladies in FLY Spirit Inc., my mentorship program, that one of the worst feelings in the world is to have sex with a man who then cheats, leaves, or never commits to you. That is truly a painful experience. At that very moment you feel degraded to a piece of meat, which then shakes your confidence and causes you to question your worth. When a man has sex with you and cheats with another woman, it causes you to doubt whether you were good enough for him. That can take a huge toll on you and can cause you to be insecure. Insecurity is when you lack confidence in and are unsure about yourself. When you become unsure of who you are, it causes you to make decisions that are beneath your value. Many people don't discuss these risks when they tell you to protect yourself during sex. Sometimes the internal damage that occurs from these types of sexual encounters can linger longer than any physical damage. A woman that isn't confident in her value is vulnerable. She is likely to do things that she said that she wouldn't in order to compensate for her lack of value.

Unfortunately, this could lead to her feeling bound to her emotions.

Many young ladies go into sexual situations seeking love and comfort but instead end up in dangerous and hurtful situations. They are seduced by the deceitful appearance. Therefore, my goal is to help women discover the root to these issues in hopes that many will avoid the traps or turn away from detrimental lifestyles. Every · woman's sexual encounters are different, but all sexual encounters outside of the original intent of sex are risky. Filling your internal voids with sexual highs is a trap. This temporary fix is a door to a house full of trouble. Fill your voids with positive things like God's words, peaceful surroundings, good friends, and purpose-driven activities. Those things open a door to a house full of grace and purpose. If you make it a habit to choose the door of grace, watch how your tendency to lean towards sexual fulfillment begins to change. I know some of this may sound challenging, but keep reading as I continue to break down how to effectively experience change and how to release all sexual residue.

# Chapter 2

# I'm The Baddest

I often sit back at times in absolute awe, thinking about the daily battle women fight internally. I can't recall ever meeting a woman that hasn't dealt with some form of insecurity at least once in their lives. Some women are approached daily with an opportunity to become unsure of themselves. It certainly doesn't help that we live in a society where women are expected to be physically flawless in order to be considered beautiful or have lots of sexual experience in order to be considered good in bed. Not to mention that it has become common to compare women with one another. As a matter of fact, I did an experiment on a small group of some of my female mentees recently, and I asked them to name the top five most beautiful women in the world. They named a few artists and actresses. Then I asked them who was the most beautiful. This caused a big debate. It was interesting to note that most of the women that they selected all have a similar body type, complexion, and sexual style. This exercise allowed me to see how my mentees defined beauty. It also allowed me to see that they think that is okay to compare beauty. However, comparison is an enemy to confidence. It causes you to think too high or too low of yourself. However, the constant female comparisons that are discussed in the media have infected our way of thinking and caused us to think that it is okay to compare ourselves with other women. Many women are now doing things - good and bad - to become highly ranked amongst society, seeking to reign supreme. It was in this spirit of competition that the term "The Baddest" was birthed.

"The Baddest" woman is one that is ranked above all the rest in terms of physical beauty, net worth, popularity, and sexual prowess. She is considered to be better than other women and is highly sought after by men. As a result, many women are working to be labeled "The Baddest" in their sphere of influence. The term has created a society where women have become extremely competitive and constantly concerned with their sexual performance and physical appearance. Ultimately, this causes many women to compromise their standards and alter their appearance in hopes that they will gain the title as "The Baddest".

Popular music, movies, television sitcoms, social media platforms and magazines often are used to nourish women's appetite to become "The Baddest". I spend a lot of time on social media, and I see multiple posts each day praising women with large butts, women whose vaginas have a particular texture, or women that are willing to perform certain sexual positions and acts. Although those posts may seem harmless, they can subconsciously frame our way of thinking if we aren't careful.

I've been blessed to mentor and influence thousands of teenage girls. It truly bothers me when I see young girls (some as young as eleven or twelve years old) posting pictures of themselves in sexual positions, claiming to be able to perform the best oral sex or to have a wettest vagina. When I see this, I always ask myself where they may have developed that way of thinking. But as I started to truly meditate on it, the answer is that it's because these types of images dominate their environments. It is so easy to get access to sexual content today. Many times you really don't have to go far to discover it. Sex is heavily advertised through our main media channels, and a lot of our cultural influencers promote sex. There are radio ads that are currently getting aired that I would have never heard as a child on a family-friendly radio station, and I am not even thirty yet.

As a child, I wasn't innocent by a long shot. In fact, I was very sexually advanced as child. I gained a lot of my knowledge from older kids, family members, and musical content. Therefore, I can relate to what this generation is going through. When I was child in the early 1990's, music had just really started to become more sexually graphic, and that was the first time I had ever heard the term "The Baddest". At the time, I truly wanted to embody that term. I wanted all the boys to praise me because I had the best body and because I knew a lot about sex. I too was looking for the voids in my life to be filled. Cell phones weren't as accessible back then, but I know that if I had a cell phone back then that I probably would have sent naked pictures of my private parts to boys. I wanted validation, just like many women and girls want today. Sexting (when a person sents a nude picture of themselves to another person via text) is an epidemic that is happening right now amongst teenagers. It's gotten so severe that the government has had to regulate it. Unfortunately, many women and girls have gotten caught up in this epidemic as they continue to seek validation.

Don't get me wrong - I don't think there is anything wrong with a woman looking her best or sexually pleasing her husband. I am totally for it and I actually advocate it. A wife's responsibility is to respect, love, and please her husband. I personally plan on doing all of that. However, I am against a woman placing her value in her physical appearance and her ability to sexually please a man. Those things can be altered or changed, but the essence of who she is makes her valuable. I am also totally against working to be of a certain sexual caliber in order to gain the praise, affection, or love of a man. He should love you for who you are. Still, I see so many women working to be the best sexually and physically to the point where they have lost their integrity in the pursuit of being "The Baddest".

I want to go ahead and issue a warning: I am going to get a little graphic for the remainder of this chapter. My goal isn't to offend anyone, but to simply shine light on some terminology and behaviors that are infecting the way some women think. I am a firm believer that we are a product of what we think, and that the things that are exposed to our 5 senses creates our thought patterns. Therefore, let's unpack some of those things.

A woman having a large butt is praised in our culture. If a woman has a small waist, nicely-sized breasts, pretty facial features, and a thick, round booty, she is considered to be a dime piece (meaning a 10 on scale of 1-10). If a woman is naturally shaped like that, there is no reason why she should not be considered beautiful. However, what about the woman that isn't shaped like that? Therein lies the problem. Because our society upholds one body type as the standard of physical beauty, women with that body type may think that they are better than others while those with a different body type may view themselves as physically inadequate. This is where women get lost in the pursuit to be labeled "The Baddest".

# Chapter 3

# The First Touch

Romance novels and movies have taught us that our first sexual encounter is supposed to be a special and significant moment with our soul mate. Christianity teaches us that our first time should be with our spouse after you have gotten married, and it's a precious moment when two people physically become one flesh. However, some women didn't get a chance to decide how or when their first time was going to be because it was forced or taken from them. Someone they knew may have touched them inappropriately or a stranger may have forced them to have sex with them. Either way, molestation and rape are horrible acts of abuse. No one has the right to sexually touch you without your permission. However, it occurs frequently. Unfortunately, it has a lasting negative impact on the victims.

Statistics show that at least 1 out of 5 women were molested as a child. While that number is very high, it only reflects those who report the molestation. There is not a school year that goes by that a young lady does not confide in me about past or present experiences with sexual abuse. We must do something about this problem. Molestation leaves a lot of women with emotional and sometimes physical damage. The residue that they are left with often haunts them for years. If they never deal with it, it can haunt them for the rest of their lives. When your first sexual encounter was molestation or rape, it can become the root to other issues in your life. Trust me, I know.

As a child I remember one of my family members ask me to grab his penis and play with him until he ejaculated. This happened once with this particular person, but that experience, along with other inappropriate encounters, triggered thoughts that affection from men would always lead to sexual touch. I thought that it was the norm. I thought that a man is supposed to sexually touch a female regardless of the age or relation. Therefore, I started to expect it, and I thought it was a symbol of love. Therefore, when certain men or boys wouldn't touch me inappropriately, I would receive that as rejection simply because of my experiences. I can honestly say that I still have to confront that type of thinking today. Although I am celibate, because I am not giving my body to men I fear that I will be rejected. When fear strikes, I have to remind myself that these thoughts are rooted in a lie. My body doesn't have anything to do with being accepted or rejected by a man that truly loves me. If a man loves me he will honor my body and not look for opportunities to take advantage of it.

Throughout life, I've met women that live a promiscuous lifestyle. Many view sexual touch as an act of love, acceptance, or pleasure. Consequently, they sleep with multiple men as a way to fulfill one of those desires. It doesn't surprise me to find out that many of those women were sexually molested as a child. Often times they don't report it, but keeping it in the dark means that they have had to deal with it alone. However, a child is not equipped to rationalize something as severe as molestation or rape. They just figure out ways to cope. Unfortunately, those coping mechanisms usually leave you with some sort of residue. For instance, failing to properly address hurt can eventually lead to a hardened or bitter heart, which can in turn lead a woman to have sex void of emotions. Although sex is a naturally emotional act for women, those with hardened hearts view it as a simple physical exchange.

The pain of being violated as a kid is often so unbearable that many people harden their hearts so they aren't able to feel anymore. It can even cause some women to develop trust issues towards the gender that molested or raped them. I know of women and girls that were molested by a woman and I know of some that were molested by a man. Molestation isn't a problem that belongs to certain gender, race, age group, or nationality; it is a worldwide problem. However, a victim of sexual abuse sometimes develops severe trust issues towards the type of person who abused them.

Because of their hardened hearts, many grow up afraid to open up to people. At times, they don't feel safe and certain things may trigger thoughts of what happened to them. These may seem like small symptoms but they can have a major impact on a person's ability to move forward in life. A person with a hardened heart often has difficulty falling in love and staying in committed relationships. A person with trust issues may have a hard time letting someone love them because they fear that people will hurt them. All of these things can be rooted in a person's sexual abusive past.

Bitterness can also harden a person's heart and cause them to lose compassion and become mean and resentful. People that have developed bitterness after being sexually abused often walk around angry at what they couldn't control, and they sometimes take their anger out on things that they can control. When I used to teach school, I remember this one particular young lady that always walked around with an attitude. She got into a lot of fights with other girls, and she always hung out with a lot of boys. The boys that she trusted used her for sex and didn't truly care about her. Consequently, she eventually started befriending more girls and eventually started to date them. I later found out that she was being raped by her mother's boyfriend and her mom knew but did nothing about it. That is why she was initially so angry with girls and showed consistent disrespect towards female authority. However, when the boys she ran to only used her for sex she ended up running back to girls for comfort, looking for the love she never received from her mother. She then began faking pregnancies for attention, until one day she finally did get pregnant. She had a child far too early in life so that she could finally have someone in her life that would genuinely love her. As you can see, this beautiful young lady's life was totally impacted by her first sexual encounter in elementary school with someone who was supposed to be a father figure.

I can go on and on with more stories that I've witnessed, heard of, or have gone through, but I think you get my point. When a woman's first encounter with sex is abusive, it is damaging. However, I don't believe that you have to remain a victim of the damage. For the rest of my life I will remain committed to doing what I can to raise awareness about sexual abuse and develop practical programs to prevent sexual abuse and help restore others that have already been victimized. Restoration and healing is possible. You don't have to live the rest of your left with the residue that you developed from being violated. Maybe I didn't even mention your symptom because there are so many different ones. But I will assure you of this: there is hope for you. If you are still being abused, the first thing you need to do is find someone that you trust and report it. Don't allow your abuser to convince you that reporting it will cause problems, that people won't believe you, or that you can destroy your family by telling someone. The truth of the matter is if you don't deal with the abuse it has the potential to emotionally destroy you. Your purpose is worth you shining the light on the dark things that are happening with you and tell the truth. If you have already gotten away from your abuser or they aren't abusing you anymore, make sure that you aren't showing symptoms of abuse. If you are, it's never too late to seek help. You might want to consider counseling or a women's program geared towards sexual abuse survivors. There are several great organizations out there that are equipped to meet you where you are. However, it no longer okay for you to walk around with this dark secret eating you up from the inside. Talking it out with a trustworthy person is liberating. I am a very transparent person not only because my life inspires others, but also because it is therapeutic. A dark sexual abuse secret is poison in your heart. Get it out! If you're not much of a talker, there are several ways to get it out other than talking. You can pray, write, or even join a support group,

No matter where you are on your journey, it is important that you begin working towards forgiveness. Forgiving the person that abused you sounds crazy, but it will help you. Yes, that person was completely wrong for what they did. However, they could have been repeating something that happened to them. That doesn't make it right, but understand that a person that takes sexual advantage of someone has their own set of issues. Therefore, forgive them. Forgiveness doesn't mean that you continue to allow someone to hurt you. If the abuse is still happening, you do need to report it. However, forgiveness does mean that you release that person and the hurt that they transferred to you, and you move forward with your life. Your sexual experiences can either be used to make you or break you. I chose to let it make me. It made me wiser and stronger, and I now use my experience to educate and inspire people everywhere I go.

Although, I forgave and I decided to move on, I still had to deal with the fact that I now had developed a sexual appetite. Even if your sexual appetite was turned on through abuse or rape, it can be difficult to turn off. In Chapter 4, I discuss how to deal with sexual desires that have been turned on prematurely.

# Chapter 4
# Turned On

If you've ever been in a building that has electricity, you are pretty familiar with a light switch. The purpose of a light switch is to turn on the lights in a particular room. The great thing about a light switch is that it requires the same amount of effort to turn off the lights as it does to turn them on. You simply reverse your previous task, and flick the switch in the opposite direction. Sexual desires also have a switch. When turned on, you develop an appetite for sexual pleasure. However, depending on how, when, or by whom your switch was turned on, it isn't always easy to turn it off.

Sexual desires were given to all of us by God. He created us to be sexual creatures. In fact, he created our bodies to physically respond to a man's touch, words, feelings, and appearance. Therefore, sexual desires aren't evil; they are natural. Nevertheless, when turned on prematurely they can create bad habits and cause you to make unhealthy decisions that can lead you to a bad destination.

I was introduced to sex at an early age. I watched my first sex scene on television when I was five years old - the same age at which I was touched sexually for the first time. Although it may sound shocking, I can actually say that my sexual switch was turned on at 5 years old. That may seem young to you, but in the community where I grew up sex was discussed regularly, and my curiosity lead to tongue kissing, humping, allowing boys to feel me up, and sneaking to watch sex scenes. What may be even more surprising to you is that I was often the aggressor who would expose boys to sexual activities. I remember one incident in fifth grade where I pulled down my pants in class and let a boy see my vagina. I would get condoms from friends and pass them out at school. Often, I would tease other students if they weren't familiar with sex. The first time I allowed a young man to perform oral sex on me was when I was about 9 years old. I reciprocated the action. Being exposed to sexual activity early created a strong sexual appetite within me.

For the next six year, I continued to feed my lustful appetite. One time didn't seem good enough. Therefore, one more time became one more. My family was totally naive to what I was doing. Some of them thought I was "fast", but they didn't know of half of the activities that I was engaging in. My mom definitely didn't know. At that age, she had a "no boyfriend" policy. My mother's didn't want me duplicate her actions and become a teen mom. But once my sexual appetite was turned on it was hard to turn it off on my own.

My sexual desires were so strong that I became addicted to sexual pleasure as a child. It was always on my mind. I looked for opportunities to be sexually gratified. I kept my virginity by the grace of God, but sexual intercourse is not the only way to be sexually pleased, and I sought that pleasure in many other ways. Sexual addiction can be just as strong as a drug addiction. They both are never satisfied, and when fed they can bring you into bondage. However, the great news is that you don't have to remain in bondage.

I gave my life to Christ in 1997, around the age of twelve. That was at the height of my addiction. By this time, I was making attempts to lose my virginity on a daily basis. I would often spend the night at friends' houses in order to meet up with boys. I attended church for years, but I wasn't making a change because I was at church doing the same thing that I was doing at home – trying to get hooked up. I joined Word Changers Church International in the mid-1990's. They had a dynamic teen ministry, and I would often go. Although, I wasn't paying attention all the time, I still heard the Word of God. Eventually, I heard enough to make the biggest decision of my life. I remember it like it was yesterday. Mrs. Stephanie Douglas asked us if there was anyone in the room that hadn't given their life to Christ yet. I knew that I never totally surrendered my life over to God, although I had numerous opportunities to do so. However, on this particular day I had a strong urge to do so. I followed that unction and gave my life Christ. I remember feeling excited leaving church that night. I jumped in the car and told my mom about the decision that I made. She was elated! That day marked the beginning of a new chapter in my life. However, I still had this sexual appetite raging within me. My spirit got saved but my body and soul were still accustomed to doing what it wanted. Therefore, there was a renewing of the mind that needed to take place. Although I gave my life to Jesus, I still wanted sexual pleasure because I had not changed my thinking. When you change the way you think, you change the way you behave. We only do what we think. So I had to start the journey of exchanging my lustful way of thinking for God's thoughts about sexual pleasure.

The best way to change the way you think is to expose yourself to information that's better than the way you currently think. The Word of God always has greater information. God created the world and you, so if you ever want to understand either, the wise thing to do is to go directly to the source. A simplistic way to comprehend the process of renewing the mind is think of a computer. A computer is designed to provide and produce only what has been downloaded onto the hard drive. You can't access software that hasn't been download to the computer. Your mind is the exact same way. Whatever has been downloaded to your mind is the only thing that you can produce or access. The downloading process may be different, but the function and impact are the same.

Thoughts are downloaded into our minds through the exposure of our five senses (sight, hearing, taste, touch, and smell) to the world around us. Therefore, if your senses aren't guarded, you can easily be exposed to information that can trigger a mental virus. Similarly to a computer, you can download a virus into your mind that will take over various areas of your life. The only way to remove a computer virus is to discover and destroy the root file. However, you have to download new security software first, which executes the removal process. Likewise, the only way to destroy a mental virus is to locate the root thought and download God's security software to help you get rid of it. God's thoughts and opinions of you and your body are your security. You can find God's thoughts concerning you in His Word. When you allow His security software to take over your thoughts, it will begin the process of eliminating all viruses. However, the law of proportions still exist. If you are spending ninety-five percent of your time feeding your mind things that produce a virus, you aren't giving God's Word an accurate amount of time to change your mind and lifestyle. If you download a virus 360 days a year and only scan your computer 5 days a year, chance of you maintaining a virus is high. What you give the most attention to will dominate your life. Renewing your mind is a daily choice. It can't be done on a few occasions. It has to be a constant commitment in order to truly be effective. That means you will have to spend time with God continually, and that's not to be extra deep or religious but to be equipped to remove all thoughts of lust and sexual immorality.

After becoming a Christian, I started my journey of renewing my mind. In the beginning it was a struggle because I was fighting against nature. However, the more time I spent with God and His Word the easier it became to resist temptation. Truthfully, I found myself still engaging in the same sexual activity from time to time although I had made a vow to be celibate. Still, I kept spending time reading and listening to the Word of God. Eventually my desire to remain a virgin became stronger and stronger. The process helped me to remain a virgin throughout school. I would later find myself in a situation where I turned my sexual appetite back on and lost my virginity at 21. However, for years my appetite was dormant. Ultimately, is it possible to be "turned-off"; however, you cannot ignore the fact that it is still a process. Don't grow hopeless or frustrated with your process. Understand that if you trying to break unhealthy sexual habits or become celibate, you may make mistakes along the way. Just remember God's grace, which is His unmerited favor, is sufficient for you. Your failures don't separate you from God. Actually, those are the best times to draw closer to Him. If you have been turned on at the wrong time, don't be discouraged, and don't become a slave to your body. Tell our body what is wise for you and make it do what you say. Don't allow your sexual desires to lead you to make choices that are attached to consequences that can't be turned off. If your sexual appetite hasn't been turned on, continue to make the necessary choices to keep it that way. Most people will tell you that it is easier for a virgin to keep their virginity than it is for someone that has lost theirs to become celibate. Nevertheless, it isn't impossible. All things are possible with faith in God. Make a quality decision to place all of your faith and hope in God and pray this simple prayer:

*God I thank you for giving me the desires of my heart. I pray that you change any sexual desires that are in my heart that aren't pleasing in your sight. Give me sexual desires that are in line with your will. I receive my deliverance from any immoral sexual cravings or appetites. Help me to have the desire to live a lifestyle that is pleasing in your sight. Thank you that your grace is sufficient for me as I walk out my process of deliverance. Thank you for your unconditional love that covers me when I fail. Help me to remain confident in your agape love for me. Thank you that I am the righteousness of God by faith in Jesus Christ, and that all of sins are forgiven. In Jesus name, Amen.*

Remember: you do not have to live in bondage to anything. You can walk in total freedom. If you are ashamed of your sexual history, don't be. Don't allow the guilt of your past cause you to live in consistent regret.

# Chapter 5

# Shameful Regret

For many years I lived with the regret of losing my virginity. After overcoming a promiscuous childhood that was triggered by both sexual curiosity and abuse, I made a decision to recommit my body to God and remain a virgin until I got married. I had engaged in sexual acts prior to making that decision, but I had been able to hold on to my virginity. However, I didn't achieve my celibacy goal. The year that I graduated from college, I gave my virginity to my college sweetheart. I remember it like it was yesterday. Once I realized that I had lost my virginity I began to cry and feel instantly ashamed. I felt like a failure. I felt like I had let everyone down, including God, myself, my family, and my future children. I wanted to set an example for my younger siblings and children to show them that that it was possible to save yourself until marriage. I didn't achieve that, and for years that was hard to bear. However, living with the shame and regret wasn't healthy for me, and it only led to me having more sex, which then led to more feelings of guilt and shame. Eventually, I realized that the shame didn't help me avoid making the same decision. In fact, it actually contributed to me repeating my negative decision. You may be currently living with some shameful regret based on sexual decisions that you have made. However, I am here to tell you that God doesn't want you walking around feeling ashamed. Shame has a way of hovering over you and making you feel less than worthy. Those feelings can lead to more dangerous ways of thinking that affect the quality of your life. Although, God wants you to live a life free from sin, He doesn't hold your failures against you. However, you may not realize that your past sexual mistakes can cause you to pull away or place distance between yourself and God. The worst place to be is distant from God. In this chapter, I will discuss some of the dangers of living with shameful regrets and how to live free from your past.

I am big on defining words. I believe that when you know the origin of words, you can fully understand them and the impact that they can have on your life. You can't stop something until you know what it is. The definition of shame is "a painful feeling of humiliation or distress caused by the consciousness of wrong behavior". The definition of regret is "feeling sad or remorseful over something bad that happened". Therefore, shameful regret is "a state of feeling remorseful humiliation caused by consciously knowing that you made a bad choice or displayed a wrong behavior". The problem with living with constant shameful regret is that you start to believe that you no longer are a good person or that you qualify for God's love and favor. Your conscience is consistently being haunted by the bad choices that you made. However, that can cause a person to become emotionally miserable and stay bound to their past. Consequently, you can't move forward in life because you are constantly living in your past. Yes, God wants you to live a life free of sexual immorality; however, He does know that all of us will make mistakes and have to receive deliverance from our sinful nature. Therefore, he provided grace for all of us to not only be forgiven of our sins but to live a life free from the bondage of sin. When you live in shame and regret you don't truly believe or receive God's gracious love for you, and that's dangerous.

Not receiving God's love and grace towards you is unhealthy. A person that doubts whether or not God loves them is a person that doesn't boldly walk out their purpose and destiny. As I have already told you, you were called to do amazing things on this earth. However, you can't accomplish those things on your own. God empowers and equips you along the way on your journey towards living a fulfilled life. But if you are still living in the regret of your bad sexual history, you won't even believe that God can use you to do great things on the earth. However, no matter what you've done please understand that God is full of new mercy and new beginnings.

There is a reason that the Bible tells us in Romans 8:1 to live a life free of condemnation. To be condemned means "to be pronounced to be wrong, guilty, and worthless". Why would God not want you to be pronounced wrong or worthless? It's because he knows that when you feel that you are worthless, you no longer make choices that reflect the fact that you have something worth living for. You begin to accept being a bad person when you're really not. You begin to stop expecting Him to do good things in your life. Therefore, you begin to settle for living a mediocre life and you continue to make bad sexual choices.

One of my favorite stories in the Bible is in the book of John. It is when some of the religious people were judging and condemning a woman that was caught committing adultery. Adultery is when an affair occurs and breaks a marriage covenant. I love the way Jesus responded to the accusations and to the woman. He told the people that they had no right to judge her because none of them were without sin. Then He extended grace to the woman and told her to be free from condemnation and go and sin no more. There are several different lessons within that story. First, maybe it's true you have engaged in sexual acts that were wrong and brought harm to others and/or their relationship. Still, nobody has the right to condemn you or make you feel worthless. Secondly, this story lets you know that God's grace is still good enough for you no matter what you've done. There is no sin that is greater than God's grace. God still wants to bless you and show His favor in your life. Lastly, after God didn't allow others to condemn her and he extended His grace towards her, He then delivered her from her sin. He told her to go sin no more, and the grace and mercy that He gave to her were the key ingredients that allowed her to live the rest of her life free from adultery. When you truly receive and understand God's love and grace, it frees you from sin.

People think that regret, guilt, and shame cause people to be delivered from committing sin; however, it actually love, forgiveness, and grace that delivers people from sexual immorality. When you recognize that God has the right to judge and punish you but doesn't do so, it gives you a thorough understanding of His love for you. When you understand His love for you it helps you recognize your value and start to love yourself. That is truly the answer to letting go of bad sexual behaviors. I know because it has worked in my life. My journey through celibacy hasn't been perfect, but God's love always strengthens me to continue. However, I did have to understand that although God's love and grace provides deliverance and forgiveness, every action still has consequences. I still had to confront things that could have or did attach themselves to me, such as soul ties, and the fear of being pregnant prematurely, and/or getting tested for STD's. Consequently, in the next few chapters we are going to discuss what to do once you no longer live in the shame and regret of your past but you still have to deal with the consequences of your actions. While some residue can be eliminated, other residue leaves behind permanent reminders. Just remember that there are blessings that come out of past mistakes.

# Chapter 6

# Soul Residue

Have you ever felt like you couldn't get over someone after you've had sex with them? Ever wonder why you can't seem to shake this particular person? It is possible that you may have developed a soul tie. Having sex is a very physically intimate act, especially for women. When having sex there is a spiritual connection that occurs that causes two spirits to become one. It was designed to be that way. God intended for husband and wife to develop a connection with one another that was unbreakable, and He used the act of sex to create that. However, a problem occurs when someone is having sex with someone that isn't their spouse. A connection is made, but what happens they are no longer involved with one another?

I have heard several women say things like, "I can't seem to get over him", "I don't understand why I can't move on from him", or "I don't think I can live without him". When I hear things like that, I immediately begin to wonder if they had sex. I believe that it harder to move on from a relationship when sex is involved than it is to move forward from a relationship where sex wasn't involved.

When I became sexually active with my college sweetheart, it became very hard to leave him or tell him no. The last two years of our relationship we were sexually active. I cried right after I lost my virginity to him, but at that moment my bond became stronger with him. I was consistently torn whenever I would have sex with him. A part of me didn't want to sleep with him, but a part of me never wanted to tell him no. I didn't want to have sex with him, because although I had messed up I still wanted to honor God with my body. However, I had this connection with him now that always moved me to say yes, even when my heart was saying no. After a while I became emotionally drained by the constant feelings of regret after having sex with him. However, the fact that he would become disappointed when I wouldn't do it made me feel guilty enough to continue doing it. During this time, we were living in the same city and even decided to get engaged. However, the soul tie that I had with him wasn't healthy and wasn't conceived in love. It was conceived in selfishness and lust. All of sudden, he found himself in a position where he had to move away from the city where I lived for financial reasons. We decided to remain a couple and be long distance. Fortunately, the best thing that can happen to someone with an unhealthy soul tie is distance. The distance between us allowed God to strengthen my relationship with Him and remove the deceptions that come along with an unhealthy soul tie. He gave me back my confidence and ability to say no to decisions that compromise my standards. While he was gone, we only had one more sexual encounter during a holiday visit. However, I told myself that would be the last time that I would have sex with him before marriage. A few months after that he came to visit me, and it wasn't long before he started to feel me up. Although I liked the way it felt, God had restored my strength, and I had the courage to resist and say no. I remember it like it was yesterday. He stopped by a convenience store to get some condoms. The entire time that he was inside the store the Holy Spirit was talking to me. He was convincing me that I didn't have to do this and that there was a better way. My heart was beating very fast. I was afraid of the repercussions of saying no to my then husband to be. As he pulled up to a hotel about five minutes away from the store, I received a text from a young lady that I mentored asking me about going to church. At that moment in the hotel parking lot, I made a choice to say no. He begged and begged and I still said no. Then he got angry with me and made me cry. Here I am planning to marry a man that gets upset with me for waiting to not have sex with him! I remember he told me that I made him waste money on the condoms he bought. It made me realize that I wasn't even worth those few dollars to him, and it made me cry even more. After a long conversation about why I wanted to wait and not have sex, he took me to get something to clean my face and then asked me if he could perform oral sex on me. WOW! That was my exact reaction. I just sat next to you and poured out my heart to you and begged you to understand my perspective, and you turn right around and ask me something like that? That is when I realized that I no longer wanted to be in that relationship. He dropped me off and then proceed to head back out of town where he lived. The next morning I woke up and went to church, and my pastor spoke a word directly for me from Heaven. He said, "There is a young lady in here who is engaged to be married. God is saying that the person that you are engaged to is really a wolf dressed in sheep's clothing. He is not who you think he is; therefore, beware." That moment really shocked me, because I knew that I had been up praying the night before asking God for wisdom and guidance. The fact that my pastor (whom I have never met) spoke those words the very let me know that it was a sign for me. I knew that God was trying to get my attention and give me the courage to remove myself from that situation.

That evening, I went home and sat my parents down and told them how I was feeling. I told them that I was considering calling off the wedding. They confirmed their own personal reservations that they had been hiding from me. I had total peace about breaking things off, but I was still afraid to do it. The soul tie that I had with him was very strong. I knew that I couldn't do it in person, because his reaction could move me to take back my decision. I knew that I couldn't allow him to talk to me for too long about the decision, because then he would try to talk me out of my decision by making me think that something was wrong was with me. Consequently, I decided to call him and explain to him that I no longer felt peace about us being together and that I no longer wanted to be in a relationship with him. That was a very difficult decision for me to make because I loved him. He tried to convince me to meet and discuss it in person, but I knew that wouldn't be a good idea. I wasn't strong enough and I could be persuaded to change my mind - not because I wanted to, but because it was hard to say no. I haven't seen him since that night that he dropped me off, and that was over five years ago. I forbade him to see me again after that day. I know that sounds extreme, but I knew how deep our soul tie was. Therefore, it was necessary to create as much distance as I could in order to fully heal and move forward from the situation.

A premature soul tie can cause problems as well. A premature soul tie is when a couple really desires to be married eventually but decides to become sexually active prior to the actual marriage. Listen, I am not saying that couples that have sex prior to marriage are set up to fail. It's possible that things can turn out to be amazing. However, I do believe that there are risks in creating your soul tie before it's time, and you can make things harder. When sex comes into play, I don't believe that you fully take the time to develop emotionally and spiritually within your relationship. You can become so enticed by the sexual experience that you don't pay attention to the other details that are important like character and integrity. The character of a man or woman is their most important attribute. Who are they? How do they handle their anger? Are they honest? Are they considerate? How do they treat people? However, a good sexual experience can cause you to neglect those vital details. Good sex is blinding. It causes you to fall for the person based on their ability to physically please you. However, physical pleasure can't compare to the pleasure of being loved by someone who genuinely cares about you. I wish more women were taught to fall in love with a man based on his character traits, integrity level, faith, beliefs, and his dedication to his purpose. Yes, I do believe that physical attraction and sexual chemistry are important in a marriage. However, I don't believe that they remove the need for the other important factors that should determine whether a person is your soul mate. Don't allow sex to cloud your judgment. You could end up putting yourself in an undesirable situation.

For instance, I have heard of several situations where a woman knew deep down inside that a man wasn't loyal or committed to her. Yet, she continued to be involved with him emotionally and sexually. For some odd reason she could not separate herself from him, and she kept responding to his booty calls. He would give her enough emotional game to convince her that there may be a chance that he would eventually fully commit to her. The game was strong enough to get her out of her panties. She continued to have sex with him, hoping and praying that he would fall as in love with the idea of being together forever as she had. However, he was just enjoying the pleasure of sleeping with her and the entertainment of having a woman around that cared a lot about him and was willing to go above and beyond for him. That was the advantage that the situation gave him. Unfortunately, he didn't intend to make a serious commitment to her. She compromised her heart, body, and future by having sex with a man that she hoped would commit. I knew that she had a deep soul tie when I realized that she knew this but still kept finding herself in the bed with this uncommitted man. If this is your situation, I'm here today to encourage you to start taking the necessary steps to be freed from an unhealthy soul tie. Here are some to get you started:

1. PRAY- Pray that God delivers you from any soul ties or spiritual connections that aren't good for you. Ask him to remove anyone in your life that hinders you from fulfilling your purpose in life. Also pray for wisdom on how to execute Step 2.

2. SEPARATE- Make a decision to remove yourself from the relationship or situation. That may mean breaking up or even relocating. Do whatever is necessary (legally) to detach yourself from any unhealthy or harmful soul ties.

3. REFILL- When you remove a major part of your life, it can leave you feeling empty. The fact that you remained in an unhealthy situation is a sign that you probably have some internal wounds that may need healing. Take time to rebuild your confidence and feed your mind with positivity. The best way to rebuild your confidence is to get in God's word and discover what He said about you. Exchanging your old way of thinking for His way of thinking concerning you.

4. GO GIRL- You've prayed, separated yourself, refilled, and healed from your past situation. Now it's time for you to go forward. Refocus your attention on your purpose and your wholeness. It's time for you to win in life. It's time for you to make sure that you become the greatness that you were designed to be. It's also time to love yourself back to a place where that good man that was destined for you can find you.

Those are four steps that can help you get free from soul ties. They truly have helped me in my life. I've been in two different relationships where there was a very strong soul tie, and I was able to get over it. These were the steps that I applied, and I saw an amazing change in my life. I pray that you gain the courage to execute them in your life and remove yourself from any situation that doesn't make you better and help you get to where you are going in life. You are worth so much more than being caught up with someone who isn't committed to you, and your body is surely worth more than giving it to someone who doesn't even understand the true value of your temple. Decide to do better today. No more soul tie residue!

# Chapter 7

# What? I'm Pregnant?

I think most women have gotten the "pregnancy talk" at some point in their life. Don't get pregnant early! Don't get pregnant before marriage! Don't get pregnant by a man that you don't intend to stay with! Those are all wise statements. I support the concept of all three; however, the question that concerns me is what happens next if one of those things does occur? Does that mean that it's over for that young lady? Is she now hopeless? Yes, her life may have tougher challenges to overcome, but does that mean that she won't be successful now? Frequently, I meet ladies that are living in regret because they are pregnant or had a child from a man that they regret sleeping with. Many get stuck wondering what they're supposed to do now. It's simple: you keeping going.

I use my platform to inspire ladies everywhere that I go. I regularly talk to ladies and encourage them to abstain from premarital sex. However, I encourage ladies that are already sexually active to work towards abstaining but to make sure that they are at least protecting themselves physically. Nevertheless, I often run into women who are practicing unprotected sex prematurely and have gotten pregnant. I also meet women who are grown but got pregnant by man that they are not committed to. They come to me seeking advice. Many times they are full of regret and disappointment. Sometimes they contemplate having an abortion or giving their child up for adoption. Others stay committed to raising the child but become hopeless. They start to believe that their dreams are over and that it's impossible to fulfill their goals.

Children are time-consuming, and having a baby forever alters the course of your life; however, it doesn't have to end your life. Don't allow your dreams to die with pregnancy, even if you got pregnant at the wrong time or by the wrong guy. In God there is always a new beginning and a new opportunity to start fresh. I am so honored to have a living example in my *SHERO*, who also happens to be my mother. My mother had me on a June day in the 1980's at the age of 16. She was devastated. She didn't want to let her parents down. She thought about how she would be judged by her peers and family. It was one of the most difficult times in her life. She had to face the fact that she did what everyone advised her not to do - get pregnant early. My mom was in her junior year of high school when I was conceived. She could have allowed her pregnancy to become the reason why she didn't finish school; however, she became determined to finish regardless. She graduated from high school and started college, only to later decide to follow her passion for cosmetology. She enrolled in and graduated from cosmetology school and went on to eventually open up her own hair salon. She has been self-employed for 20 years. She didn't allow her circumstance to stop her from living out her dreams. She knew that God called her to help build up women and their confidence. What better way to do that than helping a woman look her best. Now I would be lying if I told you that her process was easy and without challenges. It was financially tough at times and difficult finding someone to watch me; however, she didn't allow anything to stop her from achieving her goals. She was an amazing mother. She always told me that she didn't regret having me but she did regret the timing. She let me know that everything that she went through made her the woman that she is today. I look up to my mother and respect her so much.

Now, I want to take this time to encourage you. Maybe you're reading this book and you currently find yourself in an unwanted pregnancy or maybe you already had the child and things seem really tough. Please know that it is not the end of the world. The great thing about life is that we are consistently given new opportunities to make decisions that put us in better places in life. For whatever reason, your child is supposed to be here. God has a plan for their life. Did God plan the circumstances in which your child was conceived? No. However, he used that opportunity to place your child here on this earth. I am aware of the fact that there are extreme cases where a woman gets raped and conceives a child. My heart goes out to women that have had to face such a traumatic experience. Rape is a huge violation of a woman's value and innocence. Nobody should ever have to experience such pain and humiliation. Rape is an evil act, and I am just grateful that God is cable of restoring women from such horrific acts. No matter your circumstance or what you've been through, there is a new beginning in God. Children are a blessing from God even when they are conceived through an unrighteous act. You can make it through this tough time. Allow God's love to be your strength. I have met countless women who have taken on the challenge of being a teen mom, a single mom, or a mother by force due to rape, and they survived. You can too! Remain confident in God's love for you, even in those hard moments. Remember God's love for you doesn't waiver. No matter the situation, God's love and grace can turn it around for your favor. You just have to believe that. Even if you had an abortion, God is not mad at you. He will isn't for anyone to abort a child; nevertheless, he is not holding that against you. Therefore, it is time for you to stop holding that against yourself. Sometimes the number one person that we have to forgive is ourselves. I believe God has given us a blueprint of protection for life so that we can build a life that's firm, stable, successful, and beautiful, However, He understands that there will be times that we venture off from His plan. Although, that is not an excuse for us to freely venture off, it is the reason that He knows how redirect us back to the original blueprint when necessary. Therefore, understand that God's grace and love is covering you during this difficult season, and He is able to turn your entire situation around. Ultimately, make sure that you stay encouraged and receive your child as a blessing. It truly doesn't matter how they were conceived, you and your child aren't doomed. Take a situation that could be perceived as a negative and turn it into a positive. I am surely happy that my mother chose to do that. She did what it took to raise me to be the woman I am today. She was willing to work two jobs. She helped me with my homework. She introduced me to God and made me attend church. She even skipped meals sometimes so that I could have something to eat. I remember there were times that her side of the house would be cold, and my siblings and I would sleep in warmth. She sacrificed her comfort to make sure that we were comfortable. She did all of that despite the negativity of others. Despite the people that judged her for being a teen mother. Despite those who said she wouldn't be successful and that she messed up her life. My mother made sure I always knew that I was a blessing to her because God chose me. That gave me the confidence and desire fulfill God's plan for my life. Remember that your child was chosen by God. They can make a positive impact on this world. They are your gift to this world.

# Chapter 8

# He Moved On

How many times have you felt like he was the one? You're dating a guy and he just seems to be the one that you want to spend the rest of your life with. I know I can count at least five men that have made me feel that way. I looked for the opportunity to be able to feel as if the right guy had found me. In those moments, I had given my heart in the hopes of that being the reality, but each time I was let down. When your hope is consistently being let down, it makes your heart sick (Proverbs 13:12). I find that statement to be true. Nothing feels as bad as placing all of your hope in a man that leaves you. There surely isn't a feeling like placing your hope in a man that leaves you for another woman. The residue left in your heart can cause you to become bitter or doubtful. You either begin to allow your heart to harden or you begin to doubt your worth. Neither are good. There is a way to move forward from a hurtful break-up and not have harmful residue remaining.

I often tell the story of someone I dated in my early college years. I remember feeling liking there could never be another man in the world for me. I placed all of my hope and confidence in the idea that I would be his wife and the mother of his children. When he told me that I would be those things, I believed him wholeheartedly. There wasn't anything that anyone could do or say to get me to lose hope in that. However, when he decided that he didn't want to be with me anymore, that caused me to feel rejected and my heart was broken. The residue that remained with me from that situation almost caused me to take my life. Yes, I know that is extreme, but my heart was so broken and rejected that I no longer recognized my own value. This occurred with a man that I never had sex with. When he moved on from our relationship it was painful. I can't image how more painful it could have been if we were sexually active. Needless to say, I was left with a lot of harmful residue. God truly had to restore my soul. I was broken and lost. I know that there are a lot of women out there who can relate to a man that they loved leaving them. I am here to tell you that there are two ways to handle the situation. One of the ways can allow you grow and learn from the situation, and the other can hinder your growth and set you back. However, it's always our choice how we decide to confront the pain.

One way that you can handle the break- up is to give yourself time and space to heal and process. A lot times we don't give ourselves enough time to fully evaluate the entire situation, meaning understanding both parties' roles in the relationship and breakup, which aids us in removing the emotional blinders and seeing the situation for what it was. Maybe he was cheating, or maybe you just were incompatible. Assessing the relationship allows you to walk away with truths from the entire thing. However, no matter what you assess you must make a choice to learn and grow from it. If you know that you picked the wrong type of guy to give your heart to, then you can now discern when a similar type of guy is pursuing you and decide not to engage. Maybe you know that you gave him your body to early and your whole relationship was based on your sexual experiences instead of your commitment to love and cherish one another. That will make you want to save your body the next time and not give it up so easily. One thing that I can honestly say since I've been celibate most of my life is that it truly shows me how a man truly feels about me. Having a man sacrifice his sexual urges in order to honor you is one of the most honorable and loving gifts a man can give to a woman. However, sometimes you don't really learn the value of that until you've been involved with a man that didn't honor you in that way. Honey, take the lessons from your past heartbreaks and allow them to make you wiser. Become the type of woman that's not easily manipulated and tricked. Some of life's greatest teachers are failed attempts at something. Just don't allow your failed attempts to define you or your love life. There is always hope for tomorrow; therefore, forgive, love, live, and go forward. Allow this to be the way that you handle your situation instead of the following.

Allowing your break-up to break you is not the thing to do. Trust me, I know how bad it can feel to have someone dishonor, disrespect, or reject you. It is a dreadful experience. Still, when you give that experience the power to define you, you have allowed it to go too far. Never let a break-up cause you to stop caring about you. I hate to see a woman let herself go physically when she just had a rough break-up. She stops grooming, watching her weight (in a healthy manner), or taking care of her hygiene. Don't do that. Now, I am not saying that it's not okay to take a moment right after the break-up and feel the pain of the situation. Feel free to cry, feel upset, vent to trustworthy people, or write out your emotions. That is actually healthy. However, it's not healthy to stay in that place for a very long time. There is nothing wrong with getting your emotions out. Just don't let your hurt get you to a place where you to start to lose you.

Don't start doubting your worth or value, even if you were the cause of the break-up. The process still applies to those situations as well. You have to assess what happened, gain wisdom from it, and move forward. The worst thing you can do is start second-guessing who you are, because that will affect other areas in your life as well. I believe that a godly, confident, purpose-led woman is unstoppable. However, a woman that is consistently doubting her value will settle for any old life instead of reigning in life. A relationship is not the sum total of life or who you are. There is life after separations and divorce. Begin your process of allowing God to heal your wounds through prayer and communication, and set your mind to let go of the residue from your failed relationship. If he moved on, it is okay! You can move on too. If he cheated on you and moved on with the other woman, don't see that as an opportunity to get revenge or harass the other woman. I don't ever think that it is wise for a woman to go after the other woman because honestly it was the man that dishonored the commitment - not the other woman. However, I am also a firm believer that you shouldn't seek revenge on him either. Life always has a way of teaching us lessons. You just focus on moving forward and winning in your life. There are approximately

7 billion people in the world, which means that there are more opportunities to discover love. However, the key is in not placing all of your hope in a man in the first place. As humans, it is our nature to mess up. Therefore, although I trust the man that I am dating or going to marry, I don't place my trust in him. He is capable of failing me. I place all of my hope, trust, and faith in Christ. I know that no matter the outcome of any relationship, marriage, or commitment that as long as I have him and life in my body that there is always hope for tomorrow. Because of that hope in Christ, I always choose to move on.

# Chapter 9

# Recycled

Before I ever get involved with a man, I ask myself, "who am I to him?". Am I the woman he plans to build his future with? Am I the woman he just want to kick it with? Am I the woman who he only sees as a friend? Or am I another woman that he only wants sex from? It is extremely vital that I know the answer before I get involved with a man. Unfortunately, a lot a women don't find out the answer until they are already becoming who he wanted them to be in his life from the beginning. What's even more unfortunate is that some women end up being the woman he just wanted to have sex with and nothing more. At that point, you are becoming his recycled goods.

Here are a few ways to recognize if you are his recycled girl:

1. He only calls you when he wants you to come over for sex.
2. He sleeps with you occasionally but never goes out in public with you.
3. He never claims you to be anything more than a friend; however, he is consistently expecting to enjoy your benefits.
4. He only contacts you when he has just broken up with someone else.

If these are happening then there is a great chance that you are being sexually recycled. The question is: why are you allowing yourself to be recycled or why are you recycling him?

Yes, I am aware that we now live in a society where women call men for the sole purpose of sex, and often times it's the same roster of men. Whether you are recycling the same man or a man is recycling you, the root of the matter is still the same: you don't value them or they don't value you. I hear people say stuff like, "It's just sex." Honestly, it's never just sex, because sex always leads to something else. Soul ties are being developed, and usually someone catches feelings for someone. You must understand that sex wasn't created to be a meaningless act of fun. God intended for sex to be a passionate and emotional expression of love. When we try to minimize it down to a meaningless act, it never works.

People are not meant to be sexually recycled. You should never engage in that cycle. We are worth more. You are worth more. Your vagina is your jewel, and I can't tell you enough that you should make a man earn it. I know that women have strong sexual urges just like men do. But you must become a steward over your vagina and not allow any and everybody to satisfy your urge. It is extremely dangerous to do so, and like an expensive diamond, not everyone should have access to it. I love asking men who have settled down with one woman why they have done so. Often times, they offer a lot of insight. I have had several men tell me that one of the reasons they chose their woman is because she wasn't easy. Contrary to some people's opinions, there are still loyal men and women in this world. However, there are ways to present yourself in a way that demands respect. A man wants to commit to and marry a woman that he respects. When you are simply the girl that he is just having sex with, then he doesn't respect you. You earn respect from men by valuing yourself. I have met some of the biggest players in the world, and although I would never date them, I have had several tell me that they respect the way I carry myself. That always means a lot to me, because I always want to carry myself as a woman that is respected by a real man.

You can too. You can be the woman that a man respects and categorizes as marriage material. First off, if you know that you are currently in a situation where you are only a booty call, remove yourself. I understand that you may enjoy the sex that you two are having, but wouldn't it be better to enjoy sex with a man that has committed himself to you? The greatest commitment a man can make to a woman is becoming one with her in marriage. Leave that situation alone or create new ground rules. Let him know that if he genuinely wants to be with you then he needs to commit and understand you are more than your body. The sex has to stop in order for you to truly recognize how he feels about you. If he stays around once the sex stops and tries to build something real with you, then there is potential there. However, if the sex stops and then he stops contacting you, then you just did yourself a favor. You freed yourself from a man that simply wanted you for sex. Don't lower your standard to being the girl that he just has sex with. Stop going back for more in order to feel comforted or attended to. There are other ways to feel loved and wanted other than letting a man use you for sex. Just say NO to being recycled.

# Chapter 10

# Sex Trafficking

Sex trafficking is a deadly disease currently plaguing our world. I happen to be from the #1 city for sex trafficking in the United States of America: Atlanta Georgia. The thing that bothers me the most is that many of the residents of Atlanta (as well as the rest of the world) are naïve to this epidemic. I refuse to sit by and allow this to be the cause of destruction in the lives of so many people. It is sickening to know that human beings are being sold into sexual slavery where they have to give their bodies as a means of exchange. What's even more bothersome to me is that I don't believe that enough light is being shined on the problem. How is it that one of the major cities for sexual trafficking is the same city that is known as the economic boomtown of the South? Human trafficking is a billion-dollar industry, but at the cost of so many lives. No human being should have be forced to give their bodies to anyone. Sex should be a choice. I have worked with girls that have been trapped in the sex industry or rescued from trafficking. They often lose a sense of their value or place their value in their ability to perform sexually. However, you are truly are worth more than your vagina. God didn't create you to be someone's toy. A person should never feel like they can pick you up and put you down at their disposal. You are worth commitment and love. I thank God for all of the organizations that are on the ground doing what's necessary to help get these young ladies off the streets and back to safety.

Sex trafficking isn't as black and white as most think. A person can get caught up in the industry by doing everyday activities. I have heard of several instances where a young girl was kidnapped while simply walking in her community. Sometimes a person can be sold or forced into sex trafficking by people they know or have known. It is so disappointing is when I encounter situations where a woman was forced to sell her body by a sexual partner that she trusted or was in a relationship with. The young lady went into the situation seeking love and comfort but ended up in a dangerous situation. Nothing is worth your freedom, and you should never feel forced to give your body to anyone. Unfortunately, when women become emotionally dependent on a man, they are more likely to be victims of manipulation. The man uses their words and the occasional nice gesture to convince the young lady that there is nothing wrong with using their bodies to gain an "advantage". I say "advantage" because it's not always for a monetary gain. Nevertheless, it is still wrong, and it is especially wrong to be forced to do so. There is no item, currency, or status that can equal the value of your precious body. Your body is a priceless vessel of God's love. You need to become convinced of your worth, even if the sex industry has tried to rob you of it. Please know that I understand that there are women out there that feel that they had no other choice but to sell the bodies in order to provide for themselves or their families. However, I am a firm believer that there is always a greater way. I just believe that the God that I serve always provides a way of escape. However, sometimes it requires you to speak up and let people know what you're going through.

As I have surveyed my inner circle, I have come to realize that many people don't really know much about sex trafficking. For instance, I asked several people whether they were aware that the average sex slave is between 12 and 14 years old and was likely sexually abused in the past. In most cases, people are blown away by those statistics. What do you say to a young girl who has been forced to live a lifestyle that strips her of her dignity? How do you renew that young lady's mind and get her to see that she has more to offer the world than just her body? First, you have to restore her sense of value and convince her that it's not her fault. Sexual transactions are so devaluing. Therefore, the first step in helping someone recover from sex trafficking is leading them towards inward restoration.

During the season of restoration it is vital that you only speak life over them. If you are recovering from sex trafficking, you should only speak life over yourself. You don't have to wait on others to do it for you. As women we often wait on other people to encourage us or give us a compliment. However, you can do that for yourself. Find positive things about yourself and focus on those things. Also, it's vital that you look at every one of your flaws as an area where you can grow. We all have areas in our lives that we need to grow in - that's just life. However, the way you view your flaws is essential. If you already feel devalued or less than what you are, being too hard on yourself about your flaws or even the fact that you're not proud of your sexual history can be detrimental to your confidence. It's important that you learn the art of releasing your past mistakes and looking at every new day as an opportunity to grow and improve. Only speak life.

Discovering or rediscovering your purpose in life is another way to heal from the residue of the sex industry. When you know your purpose, it gives you hope for tomorrow. It gives you a sense of worth. Therefore, discovering it and becoming immersed in it causes you to shift the direction of your life. There is life after sex trafficking. You don't have to be a slave to it. You can be free. Focus on regaining your inner strength and restoring your emotions, and watch how your past hurts and pains become a launching pad to your dynamic future and destiny.

# Chapter 11

# A Woman's Worth

Women are very interesting creatures. We come in many colors, shapes, and sizes; however, that's what makes us individually unique. I've met numerous types of women, and one of the things that they all have in common is their multifaceted nature. Women can wear multiple hats effectively. God made women to be helpers, givers, mangers, nurturers, companions, wives, leaders, and mothers. The strength of a woman is admirable. They are capable of enduring trials and pains while still maintaining a high level of grace and honor. Simply put, women are beautiful spirits. However, if a woman doesn't know how valuable she is, she can become like a caged rose bush. Her growth will be limited and her beauty won't reach the height of its blossom. In a cage, she can't recognize her full potential, and it causes her to attract average opportunities. But a woman that knows who and what she is cannot be contained. Are you caged in? Have you allowed insecurities, rejection, and comparisons to cage you into a "settling mindset"? Do you settle for a fairytale date in exchange for your body as the reward? Have you settled for living a mediocre life when you were created to be extraordinary? If so, you no longer have to. It is time for you to be the greatness that you were tailor-made to be: a powerful woman with a purpose.

Ladies, you were premeditated by a perfect God. I often think about that. This perfect God that does no wrong, carefully planned and plotted you and me. He didn't have to, but he chose to. Humanity could function without our existence, but He created us to bring unique contributions to the world. I started to understand my worth when I fully grasped that concept. I was destined to be here, and so were you. Ultimately, that makes us winners.

You may not realize it, but you have been called to be a vessel of God's radiant light. He wants to shine through you. I can't tell you what your exact calling is, but I can tell you that you are called. There isn't such a thing as a human who made it to earth by accident. I don't care what mistakes you've made or where you currently are, every minute that's ahead of you is framed in hope. It's never too late to start over. I recently met a women who is living with the AIDS virus. She contracted the disease from a well-known entertainer; however, you would have never known she was living with a disease. When I met her she was smiling and full of life. She was walking around greeting everyone and very well dressed. She was a speaker at an event that I spoke and performed at. It wasn't until the middle of her speech that she revealed that she had AIDS, but she also told us that as long as she has breath she will continue to live, inspire, and educate others. Wow! That truly ministered to me. I echo her in telling you that while you are alive you need to go forward into your purpose and destiny because it's never too late. I understand that you may have been through hell, but don't let the hell that you've been through keep you trapped in your past. Get revenge on your past by moving forward into a bright future. Your struggles, pain, and disappointments are not the sum total of your life. Your determination of the outcome is the sum total of your life. Struggles are just a variable in the equation. Rise up above the bad choices, the molestation, rape, and rejection. Allow the things that should have caused you to quit on life to become your motivators. You are stronger than you think. The living God created you to be the head and not the tail; therefore, walk with your head up. Understand that you are queens, beautiful royalty. When you begin to think like that, you won't allow anything or anyone to stop you from reigning on this earth. Spend some time getting to know yourself by spending time getting to know your creator. The purpose for which you were created is within you. God wants to do a new thing in your life, but first you have to let Him. He is always willing because He feels that you are worth it. Now it's you turn to know that. Sister, you are worth it. Sometimes all you need is a fresh start.

# Chapter 12

# Fresh Start

Every fresh start begins with a decision to begin again. As human beings we make errors. It is impossible to perform perfectly, and we often have to try more than once before we get it right. There is absolutely nothing wrong with that. It's a part of life. If you have had more sexual partners than you are proud of, forgive your past and move forward. That doesn't have to define who you are. You're just one choice away from limiting your sexual partners from this day forward. I know that everyone doesn't have the same story. Perhaps you were forced to have sex and it left you emotionally scarred. Still, the same concept applies: you don't have to live with the damage of what happened to you for the rest of your life. You can be free from the torment of your past. Starting over is possible, but it's not always easy. In this chapter I will discuss practical steps that you can apply in order to create a new beginning.

## Step 1: Set Your Mind

The first step toward your new beginning is deciding within yourself that you want to change and that you are willing to do what's necessary to change. I know this step seems simple; however, it is the step that most people fail to do. You have to want to change bad enough, that you won't allow anything to hinder you from reaching your destination. You have to set your mind that you will change. Make up in your mind that you will not remain the same. Setting your mind doesn't mean that your decision to move towards change won't be challenged. People and things will try to consistently remind you of your past. Thoughts of doubt will cross your mind. Fear of the unknown will knock at your door. The fear of never finding a man that would be willing to wait for you will also try to persistently haunt you. Nevertheless, you have to recognize those thoughts for what they are: lies attempting to get you to go back on your decision to start over fresh. You have to be stubborn in your decision to remain committed to starting over and leaving your past behind. The 1st step to starting over is set your mind to do so.

## Step 2: Change Your Mind

Once you've decided that you want to change, the next thing that you have to do is challenge and change your old way of thinking. Our lifestyle is a reflection of what we think. Therefore, your past behavior was a result of how you previously thought. The only way to make sure that you don't revert back to some of those same behaviors and habits, is to make sure you uproot the thought that led to that behavior. The way you enhance your thinking is by introducing your mind to new and better content. Therefore, you have to gather new ideas, concepts, and philosophies. The best way to do that is read and listen to things that you want to become. For instance, if you want to start living a lifestyle of celibacy then you must start feeding your mind things about it. Reading, listening, and talking are the actions that feed your thinking. Therefore, you must start eating better food for thought. You are what you think about. The Bible is a great place to start. It's a great way to compare your thoughts to God's and then decide to exchange your thinking for his way of thinking. However, every book that you read doesn't have to be a religious book. Every song that you listen to doesn't have to be a gospel song. There are other great books that you can read as well.

# Chapter 13

# Heavenly Wait

Picture having sex with the man that you are in love with and having a complete peace of mind, heart, and spirit. Imagine it physically pleasing you while also spiritually connecting you with your lifetime partner. That is truly beautiful. Imagine not having to worry about whether they will stay around or if they will cheat with someone else. That's exactly what it should be like. That is what God intended it to be. God wanted sex to be a sacred thing between one committed man and one committed woman. He intended for sex to allow you to please one another physically, spiritually, and emotionally. I often hear people tell teenagers that sex is bad in an attempt to get them to not do it. However, that is very far from the truth and I believe it has the opposite impact. They know it can't be as bad as people try to portray to them because if that was the case it wouldn't be heavily promoted the way that it is in the media. Therefore, I believe the best way to educate a person about sex is to be honest with them. Sex is a beautiful thing that was created by a loving God, but its beauty is seen when you wait until marriage.

Trust me, I understand the temptation of wanting to have sex prematurely. I am currently engaged to my fiancé and we have moments that we are tempted; however, what has allowed us to abstain is our desire to honor God and wait to do it the right way. Don't get me wrong; I am extremely attracted to him, and he feels the same about me. Nevertheless, we don't want to cheat ourselves out of the gift God has for us in waiting. However, it takes two in order to carry out that decision.

Whether you are a virgin or not, there are several benefits in waiting for marriage. The bond and commitment to honor one another outweighs the desire to be sexually pleased. I feel like my fiancé and I communicate more and pay closer attention to the details of who one another are because our relationship isn't based on sex. Truthfully, our celibacy walk hasn't been perfect. We have had a few close encounters. Those encounters taught us a lot about one another. They taught us that we must maintain boundaries within our relationship. For instance, neither one of us can handle heavy make-out sessions because they're too tempting for both of us. Therefore, we do our best to avoid those types of situations. What has truly helped me stay committed to my decision to save sex for marriage is the fact that I got into a relationship with a man that shares the same willingness to wait as I do. We both would have fallen if we weren't both committed. Therefore, we decide daily to remain faithful to the commitment that we both made. Realistically, there will be moments where one of you may become weak; however, when you both are committed the other person is empowered to hold the other person accountable. One of the things that I love about my fiancé the most is the fact that he doesn't take advantage of me in my weak moments. He has used those moments to remind me of the ultimate goal, which honestly leads me back to God's will for my life. When he's been weak I've done the same for him. Who you decide to wait until marriage with plays a vital role in your success. If you are involved with someone who is looking for opportunities for you to be weak in order to take advantage of your weakness, then they probably are not the person who you should try to commit to doing this with. Don't get me wrong, I know that there have been instances were two committed people put themselves in a compromising situation and it just happened. I am aware that things happen; however, I am speaking more to the situations where there is a partner that is purposely tempting the other partner or waiting for the chance to get them to have sex prematurely. If this is the type of person you are with, you need to sincerely ask yourself whether you truly want to be with them. If they can't honor your desire to wait and honor God, what makes you think that they will honor any of your future wishes? I believe many women think that they have the power to change a man. However, contrary to your way of thinking, the only person that can change the way a man thinks is himself and God. A person must first decide that their thinking is wrong before they can be convinced that it needs to change. Consequently, you have to make a decision not to date someone who isn't morally and spiritually like-minded. Don't rob yourself of the heavenly sexual experience that God has for you because you settle on your companion or don't believe that you are worthy of the wait. There are several amazing benefits to waiting to have sex until marriage, and I want to highlight seven of them:

7 Benefits to Saving Sex until to Marriage

1. **You Value Having Sex with Your Spouse More**
   This is very true. When you wait to have sex with your spouse within the framework of your marriage

you value the experience more. It is likened to that car that you really desired but you had to save up for a year to buy. When you finally get that car, you are less likely to be reckless with it. You'll have the car cleaned on a regular basis, and you are less likely to take driving risks in your car. Why? Because you know what it took for you to get that car and you value it. Likewise, when you wait to have sex with your spouse, you are less likely to take advantage of your spouse physically. You appreciate your sexual experiences more. Sex means a lot to you when you are married. You'll also think twice before doing something to jeopardize your union because you recognize the investment that you put into it. Sexual encounters become more meaningful when you wait until marriage.

2. **You Develop Discipline Within Your Union**

It requires a lot of discipline to abstain from sex with someone that you are romantically involved with. However, when you exercise and develop sexual discipline within your relationship, it helps you prepare to be disciplined in other areas in your relationship and in life. For instance, my decision to abstain from sex has helped me develop the ability to say no to my body when it is craving sexual fulfillment. That is significant. In marriages, there will be times that your spouse won't be able to have sex.

They may be out of town, busy, tired, or physically unable to perform. However, those are times when your discipline will kick in despite what your body desires. Yes, you have a choice to fulfill your sexual desires selfishly and do things that are outside of your marriage commitment, but the consequences can jeopardize your union. Also, it doesn't just help you develop sexual discipline, it helps you as a couple develop discipline to stay committed to a decision that you've made together. Therefore, when you have to be disciplined when it comes to your finances or any other area, you are equipped to remain faithful to your choice. Developing discipline within your union is beneficial on so many levels. It is truly worth it and will give you the advantage throughout the course of your marriage. Therefore, saving sex until marriage has benefits that can last a lifetime.

3. **You Avoid Having Children Before You're Better Equipped To Parent Them**

As I discussed earlier in the book, there is life after an unplanned pregnancy. I believe that life can still be great and your children can still grow up to be extremely successful. Nevertheless, there is an advantage in placing yourself in a better situation before giving birth to children. Although you can't predict life or mishaps, you can plan to be a little better prepared for things. When you wait until marriage to have sex, you give your child a higher chance of growing up in a household with both of their parents. It is becoming more common to grow up in a house with only one parent even though that is not God's best for us. We know that there are several advantages of having two loving parents working together to raise a child. I believe that the home life of a child has a large impact on how that child views life and family. Not to mention the economic demand that it requires to raise a child. It definitely helps when you can be in a financially stable condition before having children. Although children come with unexpected expenses, you can position yourself to be ready for them. Trust me, a single parent raising a child on one income and no emotional or financial support from a spouse will tell you that if possible they would welcome the opportunity to do it the right way with a spouse. Saving sex until marriage allows you the opportunity raise your children the way God intended for them to be raised - with two loving parents.

4. **You Develop a Deeper Sense of Trust**

Trust is essential in maintaining a healthy marriage. It is impossible to have a happy marriage when there is a lack of trust. Believe it or not the fact that I abstain from sex with my fiancé is one of the reasons that he says that he trusts me more. He doesn't worry about me sleeping with another man because he knows that, despite my desire to be physically intimate with him, I abstain in order to honor God and him. My willingness to wait until marriage develops trust with my future spouse. I trust him more with my heart, body, and soul because he honors me in such a way. I have lowered my guard with him because of his willingness to honor the God in me. Many people don't understand how saving sex until marriage actually brings you closer to your partner. I love him more because we are waiting. Every time we have the opportunity to go back on our choice and we decide to remain committed, my love seems to grow deeper for him. In this way, abstaining builds trust within your relationship.

5. **You Will Have Built a Stronger Foundation of Friendship**

I often hear married couples say that the romance comes and goes in a marriage, but having a genuine friendship means that you still love and respect one another when it's absent. Having sex before marriage puts the focus on sexual fulfillment instead of on getting to know the other person. A great part of developing a friendship is learning as much as you can about the other person and falling for them because of who they are instead of how they please you. Contrary to popular opinion, marriage isn't about being pleased. If anything it's about pleasing and giving your partner the advantage. Love gives! If both partners focus on loving their spouse, then both people will feel loved. It is about bringing your strengths to your partner's weaknesses (and vice versa) so you can help eliminate them. When you and your spouse have a solid friendship, you are better equipped to fulfill the will of God for your lives together. However, it's impossible to know their strengths and weaknesses if you don't know them, and the best way to get to know them is to be friends first. When you build a friendship without sex, you'll pay more attention to and better understand your mate. The conversations that happen when sex isn't in the picture truly build the foundation of your union. When sex isn't an option, you create other ways to express your love for one another. Don't rob yourself of the opportunity of truly becoming friends with him. If you really take the time to become friends with him, you'll build a stronger foundation to stand on throughout your marriage. Premature sex will stunt your growth as a couple. Don't get involved physically and hinder the spiritual and emotional growth that occurs in the friendship phase.

6. **Display a Great Example for Your Kids**

   I often hear adults justify their decisions based on what their parents taught them. They place a lot of weight on what their parents have raised them to believe. It doesn't matter if the information was true or not. They hold certain things to be true simply because their parents said it or did it. That lets me know that parents are a child's first role models. Unfortunately, I don't think that parents always are conscious of that. Allowing yourself to be the example for your children by saving sex until marriage means that you'll have a wonderful lesson that you can teach them later. While I do understand that children have their own mind and will make their own decisions, it cannot be denied that knowing that their parents were able to abstain until marriage gives them hope that they can accomplish the same thing. Saving sex until marriage allows you to be a great example for your future children and makes it possible to start a new trend in your family. However, even if you are currently married and you didn't wait, you can still be an example for your children and lead them down the right path. Your voice and advice matters to your kids.

7. **You Honor God**

Sometimes I think that people forget that God is more than a supernatural being, He is a father. We are God's daughters. God created sex for reproduction and to be a pleasurable gift to man and woman. However, just like an earthly father, God wants to make sure that whomever you give your body to wants more than just sex from you. God wants them to genuinely love, respect, and honor you. God honors us in so many undeserving ways. He is consistently blessing us, giving us grace, and showing his unwavering love. When I think about God's goodness, it makes me what to honor Him. The fact that nothing I do stops Him from blessing me and loving me makes me want to honor him more. When you truly have a personal relationship with God, it is hard to be comfortable doing things that he doesn't want you to do. Honestly, I truly wouldn't benefit from having sex with my fiancé prior to marriage. Although it may physically be gratifying, I will not be totally satisfied. My soul would constantly be reminded of the fact that there is a better way, and that creates internal unrest. Saving sex until marriage brings a peace that can't be described. That is because there is a peace in knowing that you are doing it God's way. You'll be able to have peace in making love to your husband instead of having sex before marriage and having the thought in the back of your head that God isn't being honored in the moment. Therefore, I believe that it's beneficial to save sex until marriage because it helps you honor God with the body that He created for His glory.

Sex is beautiful thing. When done right there is nothing that can be compared to it. When you want to know how something operates at its fullest potential you go directly to its creator. Therefore, since God is the creator of sex, it would be ignorant of us to allow other creations to tell us how the creator created something to operate. God knows the ins and outs of sex and how it is supposed to be done. Don't allow your finite knowledge to cause you to think that you know more about sex than God. The best sex is sex that is done the way it was designed to be done. I know that society has an opinion about sex and how it should happen, but I have witnessed the imperfections and consequences of their advice. Therefore, I choose to rely more on God's advice concerning sex. Sex is at its greatest within the framework of marriage. Don't fall into the trap of thinking that you are missing out on something when you wait. That is a lie, and the opposite is actually true. You miss out on a heavenly experience when you don't wait. Don't rob yourself of that experience. You are beautiful, amazing, one of a kind, and valued. You are worth the wait. You are worth the sexual experience God created for you. You are worth living without negative sexual residue. You are worth all of the benefits of saving sex. You are worth the heavenly wait.

# Chapter 14

# Who, Me?

You are important to this world. I don't care about your past, your failures, your sexual residue, or your hurts. None of those things take away from that fact that you are significant. The reason that I said that I don't care is because neither does God. God isn't apologetic about creating you. Neither has He repented for giving you an important purpose. You have a God-given purpose. God created you to solve a problem on this earth. You have to be confident in that and know that you matter. In fact, your significance is probably why you have experienced some of the hell that you've been through. Some of the most powerful people in the world have had to overcome some of the toughest situations in life. However, you can look at it this way: the mere fact that you overcame it lets you know that God still has a plan for your life. Every day that I wake up, I know that God must still have something for me to do. I didn't have to wake up today. The things that I've gone through could have caused me to lose all hope and desire to live. I could have taken my life the numerous times that the enemy tempted me to do so, but something just wouldn't allow me to do so. Now I know that that something was God. Don't give up on you! The best way to let go of all of the sexual residue that has attempted to keep you bound and hindered is to become focused on achieving the purpose that God created for you to accomplish. I am not naïve to the fact that many of you may not know your purpose, and I have dedicated this last chapter to helping you begin to discover it.

First, I need you to understand that you have a purpose and that no matter how old you are it's never too late to fulfill start fulfilling it. God does everything on purpose and for a purpose, and the fact that you are still alive lets me know that He is purposely allowing you to be here. It is time for you to shake off all of the residue and move boldly toward your future. Your future is bright and exciting. It's not perfect, but it is better than your past. How do I know? Because you are only one decision away from not allowing your past to define your entire life. We decide whether we are going to be victors or victims.

I've been molested, I've been cheated on by a man I was committed to, I lost my virginity to someone who lied to me, and I've had to take pregnancy tests in fear of becoming a mother before I was ready. Still, I have decided that I will not look like what I've overcome. I will not be defined by things that were meant to destroy me. I choose to be the greatness that God designed for me to be. You can too! Don't underestimate your strength. Women were designed to be strong individuals who can adapt in any situation. You are stronger than you know. It is time for you to forgive your past and embrace your future. When we don't forgive our past we give it the power to hold us captive. You've already had to endure the pain of it once. Don't allow it to consistently keep you yoked with the pain so that you have to relive it over and over again. If you are currently in any danger, please reach out to the appropriate personnel to assist you in getting the aid that you need. We have listed a few resources in the back of the book. However, you need to decide that you are going to turn the page and enter a new chapter of your life. That doesn't mean that you will forget the previous chapters, but it does mean that you don't have to continue carrying the residue of the past. As I stated earlier, the best way to start a new chapter is to get focused on your purpose.

You don't truly know your purpose until you know who created your purpose. Having a personal relationship with God is the best decision I have made and the best one you can ever make. I truly wouldn't be who I am today without Him. He is the one that healed my heart from the pain of everything that I endured. The thing that I love about God is that He accepted me as I was and He changed me. I didn't have to change myself or figure everything out. I couldn't even if I tried. All I did was stay committed to the process of getting to know Him and His thoughts towards me. The more I got to know Him and how He felt about me, the more I began to learn about myself. The more I learned about me, the more that I learned that I was important to Him. Spending time with God is where He revealed my purpose to me. I realized that I was I was truly designed and tailored by God to do what He called me to do. My personality fits my purpose. My upbringing fits my purpose. My trials and the things I had to overcome prepared me for my purpose. Now I am a firm believer that God doesn't cause bad things to happen to us; however, I do believe that He uses those things and turns them around for our good. Therefore, I invite you to develop a relationship with God right where you are and as you are. I also want you to answer a few questions that may lead you in the right direction towards discovering your purpose:

1. If you could solve one problem on earth, what would it be and why?

   _____

   _____

   _____

   _____

   _____

   _____

   _____

   _____

2. If money wasn't an option, what job would you do for free and why?

   _____

   _____

   _____

   _____

   _____

   _____

   _____

   _____

   _____

3. What is something that you are very good at doing and can do with ease?

_____

_____

_____

_____

_____

_____

_____

Typically, the problem that people are the most passionate about is the problem that they hold a solution to. For instance, I hate seeing women insecure and unsure of themselves. I also hate to see women be sexually abused or used. Those are the problems that bother me the most. It doesn't mean that other problems aren't just as significant, but those are the ones that touch my heart the most. Consequently, that also my purpose. God uses me to empower young women and girls. I would do that for free. I actually have times where I still do it for free. My nonprofit organization has been established since 2010 and I've never collected one paycheck from it. However, I still meet with the girls I mentor on a weekly basis. I have had jobs that paid me to do my passion, but I know that it's my passion and purpose because I am willing to do it for free.

Remember God is the most purposeful being ever. He will not give you a purpose and not give you the grace and skill to do it naturally. Your natural gifts are tied to your purpose. What is it that comes naturally to you and has an impact on the world and people? For me it's inspiring and entertaining people. Everywhere I go people tell me that I inspire them and encourage them, but it comes naturally to me. I hate to see people discouraged. If I could have it my way, everybody would be happy. Therefore, I'm always doing things to help people. What is the thing that comes naturally to you that will leave a positive mark on the world or the people in it? It doesn't have to be anything like serving people. You could be the person that's so analytical that you end up inventing the next big thing that makes all of our lives easier. I don't know exactly what your purpose is, but I do know that God does and that you have one. I want to encourage you today to embrace your purpose and be determined to not allow anything from your past to stop you from fulfilling your purpose. Ladies, shake off the sexual residue today, and walk into the awesome destiny God has for you. Declare it over your life today: No more residue. #Residue

# ABOUT AUTHOR

**FLY is a Hip-Hop Artist, Actress, Author, Motivational Speaker, and Radio Personality who brings substance and a pristine flavor to the entertainment industry.**

**FLY Musiq**, a multi-talented, soulful, and lyrically gifted Atlanta native, was born on a beautiful summer day into a world that cultivated her musical growth. An artist since the age of 5, she experienced a plethora of musical genres throughout her upbringing. Her experiences have granted her the ability to float gracefully between hip hop and soul, crafting a sound that is uniquely hers.

Her name comes from her passion and desire to share the message of faith, love, & youth, hence her name– FLY. Her purpose is to deliver music that penetrates and restores the soul. She desires to express her love for God, life, and people through her music.

In June 2013, FLY published her first book, "Recognize Your Fly," a book focused on helping individuals identify what they were born to accomplish and who they are destined to reach. FLY also is a highly sought after motivational speaker, who has spoken to over 100, 000 youth across the country..

Thousands have been moved by FLY's live performances. She's had the esteemed honor of performing at Coretta Scott King's 85th Birthday Celebration/Freedom Concert and at many other historic Atlanta venues and events. in TRIBES Magazine.

FLY has teamed up with One Billion Rising, a global initiative to end violence against women. She and Sam Collier penned the song 'Rising' and released a music video for the track as a tribute to the women and girls affected by violence. On Valentine's Day 2013, the two performed the song for over 20,000 people at the Georgia State Capitol as a part of the organization's One Billion Rising Day.
While FLY continues to grow as an artist, her success is not exclusive to music and acting as she exhibits her ability to captivate audiences through her abilities as a savvy businesswoman She is the founder of

FLY Musiq Group LLC and FLY Spirit, as well as the co-founder of Love Redefined LLLP. FLY Spirit is a youth mentoring program that empowers young people to "FLY" above all obstacles.

Even with such an extensive resume' that spans the business, acting, music, speaking, and nonprofit worlds, FLY refuses to rest on her laurels. October 2013 was the release of FLY's third EP entitled 'Evolution FLY', which she describes as a musical biography of her life's struggles and victories. On the same day of her album release, she also released 'Redefine Beautiful', the masterfully written follow-up to her first book 'Recognize Your Fly' that encourages people to abandon their skewed definitions of beauty and see themselves through the eyes of the only one that really matters – God.

And because FLY's passion for people knows no bounds, she will soon be extending her message of faith, love, & youth to the arena of visual arts with her forthcoming 'FLYTASTIC' comic book series. While the concept of having a female character at the forefront of a comic empire is virtually unheard of, 'FLYTASTIC' will show the world that love is a powerful force that makes all things possible.

FLY is a woman that aims to make a positive mark on the world that can never be erased, through her gifts and talents.

www.flymusiq.com

Facebook: FLY Musiq

Twitter: @flymusiq

Instagram: @flymusiq

YouTube Channel: OfficialFlyMusiq

39770487R00068

Made in the USA
Charleston, SC
19 March 2015